Usborne Fantasy Puzzle Books

King Arthur's Knight Quest

Andy Dixon

Illustrated by
Simone Boni

Edited by
Felicity Brooks

Cover and additional design by
Stephanie Jones and Amanda Gulliver

Additional editing by Claire Masset

This edition first published in 2010 by Usborne Publishing Ltd, 83–85 Saffron Hill, London EC1N 8RT, England.
Copyright © 2010, 2005, 1999 Usborne Publishing Ltd.
The name Usborne and the devices ♀♀ are Trade Marks of Usborne Publishing Ltd. All rights reserved. No part of this publication may be reproduced, stored in any retrieval system, or transmitted in any form or by any means, electronic, mechanical, photocopying, recording or otherwise, without the prior permission of the publisher.
UE. Printed in China. First published in America 2010.

MISSING
Have you seen these knights?

Sir Lomvert   Sir Swinage   Sir Aquatane

Sir Gawain   Sir Tripont   Sir Larbre

Sir Nocturne   Sir Heronbow   Sir Galahad

Last seen leaving Camelot Castle on various quests.
It is believed that they have had evil spells cast upon
them by Morgan le Fay and are now in mortal danger.

REWARD FOR THEIR SAFE RETURN

GRAND TOURNAMENT

Tuesday, 12 noon on
Camelot Field

(Games in Great Hall if wet)

King Arthur,

I have kidnapped
your knights and
I'll never return
them.

Ha, ha, ha

**Morgan
le Fay**

Win yourself the opportunity to rescue the Knights of the
Round Table by entering the Grand Tournament.

Three lucky winners will get the chance to go on a quest
to save the knights and defeat Morgan le Fay, the wicked
sorceress thought to be responsible for their disappearance.
Anyone who completes the quest successfully will be
made a Knight of the Round Table.

Do you have the courage, wisdom and
strength to be one of the chosen few?

By order of:
Arthur Pendragon,
King of Logres

Information for knight rescuers

Thank you for volunteering to rescue King Arthur's knights and welcome to Camelot, the most wonderful castle in the Kingdom of Logres. Before you set off, there are a few things that you need to know, so please study these pages carefully.

What am I doing in Camelot?

You have been offered a chance to go on a quest to rescue the Knights of the Round Table.

Why do they need rescuing?

Because King Arthur's enemy, the powerful sorceress Morgan le Fay, has cast spells on them so that they cannot return to Camelot. The kingdom is in crisis and the sorceress must be stopped before she seizes the throne and declares herself ruler.

Do I have to go by myself?

No. King Arthur has organized a tournament to select the others to go with you. Each knight that you manage to rescue will also join the quest. Together, you should be powerful enough to defeat Morgan le Fay.

Is the quest dangerous?

Yes, but if you succeed, Arthur will make you a Knight of the Round Table – a great privilege.

How will I recognize Morgan le Fay?

She looks like this picture.

What exactly do I have to do?

Win a place on the quest at the tournament, then set out from Camelot and travel to Morgan le Fay's Castle, rescuing knights along the way. In each place you visit, you will see a picture similar to the one below. One knight needs rescuing in each place. The frame around the picture contains all the information you need.

This tells you where you are in the Kingdom of Logres.

When you have left Camelot, you will see *a shield* in each place you visit. It belongs to the missing knight and shows his coat-of-arms. The sorceress has used her magic on the knight in a way that is linked to the coat-of-arms. Look carefully at the shield and it will help you to find the knight.

The *pieces of parchment* tell you what you have to do in each place that you visit. There are puzzles to solve and things to do.

Demon's Bridge

There's *one piece of knight's equipment* (golden weapons, spurs, a breastplate etc.) hidden in each place you visit, including Camelot. The picture shows what to look for. The complete set of equipment is magical. Whoever wears it will be protected from evil when you reach Morgan le Fay's castle.

In each place you go to a *map* shows you where you are in the Kingdom of Logres. The map on the opposite page shows the whole kingdom.

Merlin's crystal ball shows clues to help you solve the puzzles. Merlin is Arthur's wise magician. He can't come with you because he must stay to protect Arthur, but he'll give you his crystal ball and appear in it with a clue when you need help.

There's *a golden chalice* hidden in each of the first nine places you visit, including Camelot. You'll need all of the chalices later when you meet Morgan le Fay, so don't forget to look for them.

The Grand Tournament is about to begin at Camelot. When you have studied the map of the kingdom, turn the page to find out who will be going with you to rescue King Arthur's Knights...

THE KINGDOM OF LOGRES

Castle le Fay

Fool's Lake

Druid Stones

Green Chapel

Swine Hill

Demon's Bridge

Raven's Wood

Dark Mountains

Pendragon Beacon

Camelot Castle

N
W   E
S

The Camelot Tournament

Welcome to the tournament to find the people to rescue King Arthur's knights.

The winners will be those who can find a red handkerchief hidden among the trees and present it to the king. Three have already been found. You must find the fourth before anyone else can, and spot which contestants have the other three.

Merlin has a gift that will help you to overcome Morgan le Fay's evil magic. It is a crystal ball that allows you to see Merlin (though not hear him). To prove you are worthy to use it, you must find Merlin and the crystal ball then solve this riddle:

"What can you feel but cannot touch?
What can whistle but has no lips?
What can move trees but cannot be seen?"

7

Raven's Wood

The first place you visit on your quest is Raven's Wood. Deep in the woods you are attacked by ravens. They think you have come to steal their eggs, which have fallen out of their nests.

To calm the ravens, find seven eggs and an empty nest to put them in.

Hal Hirsuit

Lady Lionheart

There are two mushrooms growing in the woods, one good and one bad. If you feed the knight the good mushroom, he will be freed from Morgan le Fay's spell. If you feed him the other, he will remain a prisoner of the woods forever.

With Merlin's help, find the good mushroom. Then find the missing knight and feed it to him.

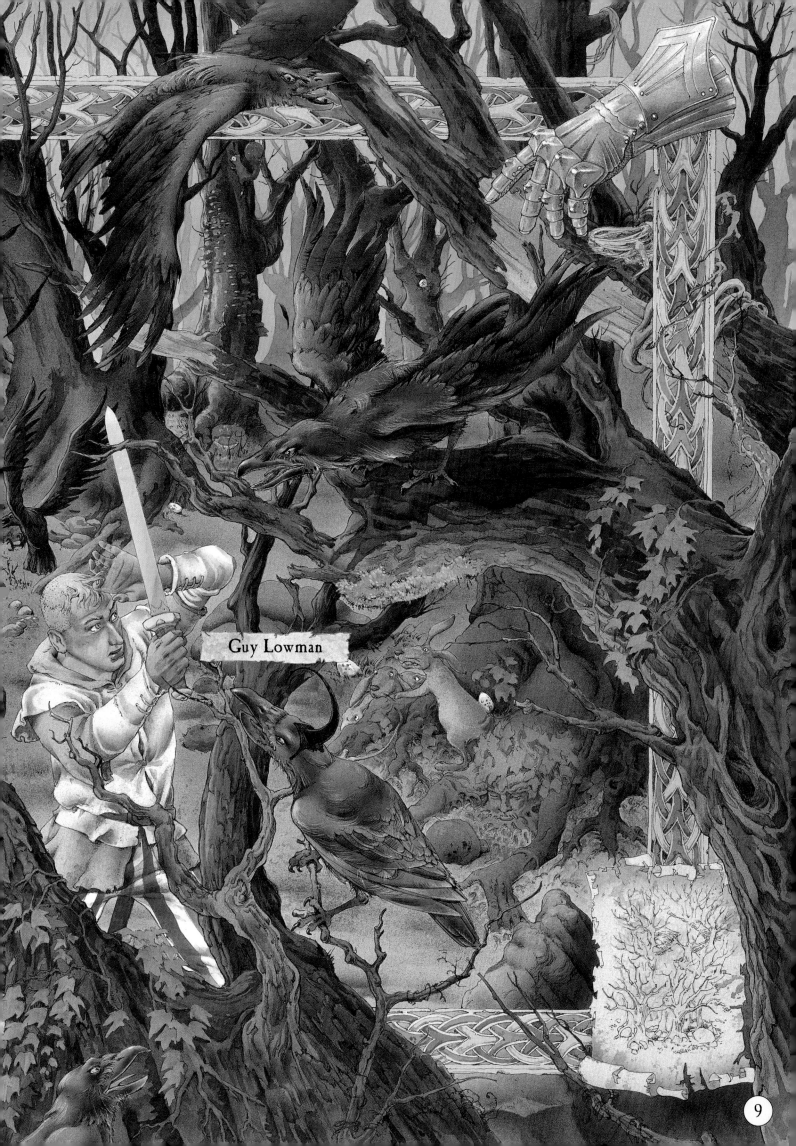

Guy Lowman

9

Swine Hill

Beyond the woods, on top of a hill, you reach a settlement of pig farmers. They are suspicious of strangers and start to attack you with stones. To show them that you mean no harm, you must find the sacred pig stone and kiss it.

You can identify the bewitched knight by the mark on his body which is different from any other you can see. To free him from the spell, you must find the magic bronze nose ring and place it in his nostrils. Take care – there are many rings in Swine Hill. If you choose the wrong one, the knight will eat pig food for the rest of his days.

Demon's Bridge

Your route is blocked by a fast flowing river, so you must use the Demon's Bridge. Each knight on the bridge guards a different path. One is a powerful warrior from whom it would be impossible to escape. The other is made of stone and is harmless. Find out which is which and cross safely.

Now find Arthur's missing knight and raise him safely to the level of the bridge, using the winch. To operate the winch, first you need to find the winch handle.

You can unlock the knight's cage by turning the correct fish key in the mouth of the fish. Be careful – if you choose the wrong key the knight will fall to his death on the rocks or into the icy water.

The Green Knight

You've reached the Green Knight's Chapel, where the Green Knight challenges you to exchange weapon blows with him. He has the power to replace his head after it has been cut off.

Demand to strike the first blow and then hide his head under the serpent's tail before he can replace it.

The missing knight has been beheaded, but all is not lost.
There is a magic belt hidden in the chapel. Find the knight's
head and body, place the head on his shoulders and wrap the
belt around his neck. The knight will come back to life.

Beware! There are two magic belts. Only the Evergreen
Belt will give life, the other kills all that touches it.

Fool's Lake

At Fool's Lake you are taken prisoner by a colony of jesters and clowns. Their leader demands that you roll the dice of death. There are three dice to choose from. You will only be allowed to go if you choose the correct one. By looking carefully at the leader's scroll, you should be able to find out which it is.

King Arthur's knight has been turned into a clown. Many of the clowns carry sticks with models of their own heads on top. Study all the sticks carefully and you should be able to tell which of the clowns is really the knight.

The knight can only be released from the spell through the power of his own tears. When you have found him, you need to find a way of making him cry to break the spell.

The Ferryman

Your next mission is to rescue a knight who is chained to a tree on an island in the middle of the lake. The ferryman will take you there if you solve his riddle: "My bear wants to eat my wolf and my wolf wants to eat my hens. How can I get all my animals safely across to the island, if I can take either the bear or the wolf or the hens in my boat on each crossing?"

The knight's chains are secured with an unbreakable lock.
The Lady of the Lake holds two keys. Only one will open
the lock and free the knight.

If you touch the wrong key, the ferry and everyone aboard
it will be sucked down to the bottom of the lake. If you
choose the correct key, you will be allowed to cross safely
to free the knight from his chains.

Dragon's Cave

An opening in the side of the hill on the island has led you to a cave where a huge dragon lies asleep. If you disturb it, it will eat you and spit out your bones.

The dragon is blocking the main path, so you must find another way across the stones. Don't step on any with bones on them. If you rattle one, you'll wake the dragon.

The knight is imprisoned in one of the towers. You can't call to him or you'll wake the dragon, and you can't see inside the towers. Two towers are open. Inside one is the key to the knight's prison. With Merlin's help, find which tower contains the key and choose a path to reach it. Then find out which tower the knight is in and select a safe route to get to it. If you go into the wrong tower, the door will slam shut and you will be prisoners forever. Once you have rescued the knight, you must find a route out of the dragon's cave.

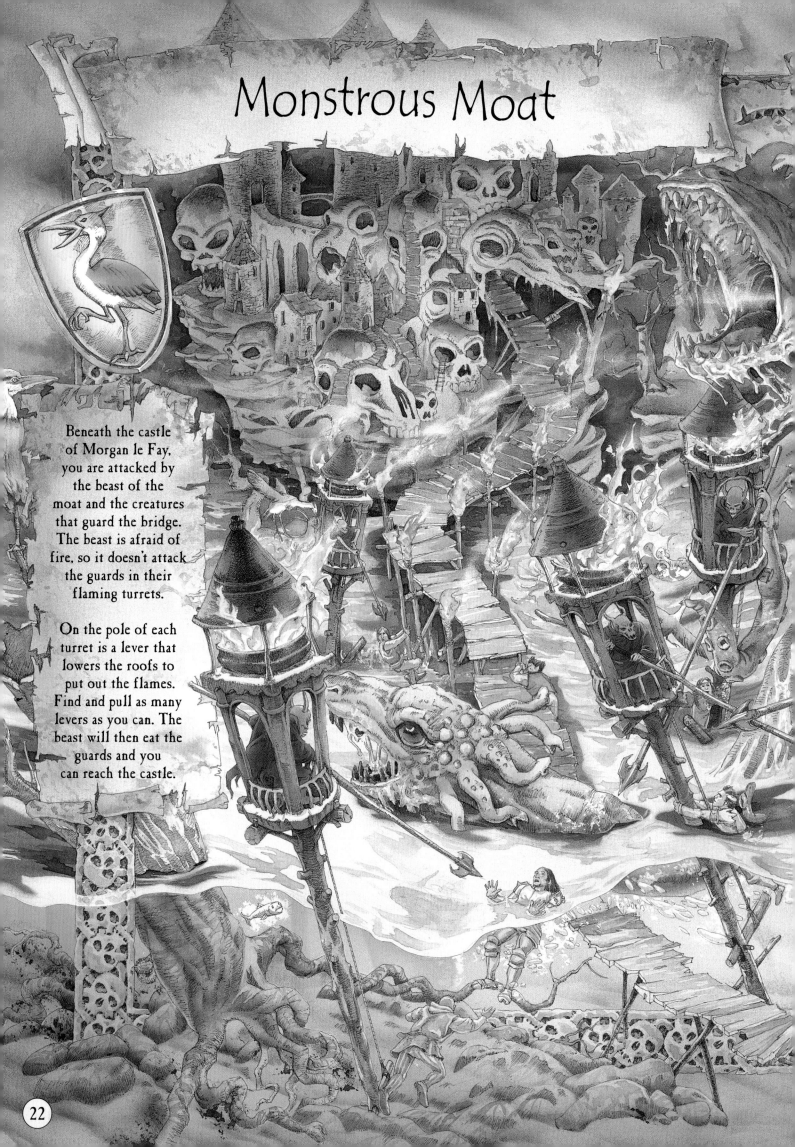

Monstrous Moat

Beneath the castle of Morgan le Fay, you are attacked by the beast of the moat and the creatures that guard the bridge. The beast is afraid of fire, so it doesn't attack the guards in their flaming turrets.

On the pole of each turret is a lever that lowers the roofs to put out the flames. Find and pull as many levers as you can. The beast will then eat the guards and you can reach the castle.

The knight has been turned into a heron. There are a few of these birds around the moat, so you will need your wits about you to find the right one.

To release the knight from his feathery fate, first catch the fish that glows and feed it to him. You cannot touch the fish or its power will vanish, so you must find something to catch it with.

The Sorceress

Inside her castle, Morgan le Fay is about to sacrifice Sir Galahad in a fire that rages from under the Earth. You're losing the battle against her guards, so you must find the magic golden sword that completes the knight's equipment. When your companion has the sword, he'll be able to destroy the guards and stop them from throwing Sir Galahad into the flames.

The nine chalices you have collected on your journey have become scattered around the vaults, along with one other. Recover them all and place the chalice shown on Sir Galahad's shield in one of the eight shrines below the sorceress. If you choose the wrong shrine, the sorceress will destroy you in the fire and the kingdom will be doomed. If you choose correctly, Morgan le Fay will be consumed in her own evil fire and the kingdom will be saved.

The Round Table

Congratulations! You have saved all of King Arthur's knights and rid the kingdom of the evil Morgan le Fay.

The king has set places for the nine knights and for you and your three companions at the Round Table. Can you find out who sits where?

Merlin has discovered a marble stone magically floating in the river. Stuck into the stone is a fabulous sword with this inscription on its blade: "Whoever solves my riddle can withdraw me and sit at the king's left side: 'Find a beast in a circle of light. The living beast wears a symbol. The woven symbol hides my twin. Excalibur is its name. Return it to the king.'" When you have found Excalibur, you can draw the sword from the stone. King Arthur can knight you and your companions and you can take your place by his side as a Knight of the Round Table.

The Camelot Tournament 6-7

Golden shield 1

Chalice 2

Red handkerchiefs
3 4 5 6

Merlin and the
crystal ball 7

Riddle answer: the wind

Raven's Wood 8-9

Golden gauntlet 1

Chalice 2

Missing knight:
Sir Lomvert 3

Nest 4

Eggs 5 6 7 8 9 10 11

Good mushroom 12

Bad mushroom 13

Swine Hill 10-11

Golden helmet 1

Chalice 2

Missing knight:
Sir Swinage 3

Pig stone 4

Nose ring 5

Demon's Bridge 12–13

Golden breastplate 1

Chalice 2

Missing knight:
Sir Aquatane 3

Living warrior 4

Stone warrior 5

Winch handle 6

Fish key 7

The Green Knight 14–15

Golden spur 1

Chalice 2

Missing knight:
Sir Gawain's body 3,
Sir Gawain's head 3A

Serpent's tail 4

Evergreen Belt 5

Wrong belt 6

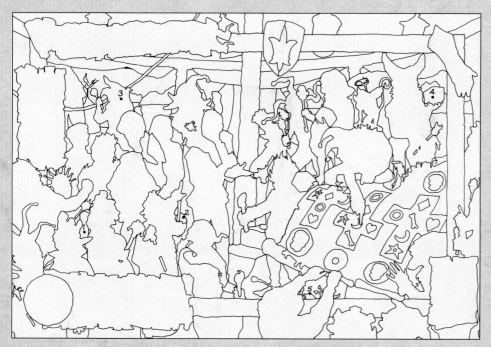

Fool's Lake 16–17

Golden gauntlet 1

Chalice 2

Missing knight:
Sir Tripont 3
(his clown stick is
a knight's helmet)

Correct die 4

Onion 5
(to make the knight cry)

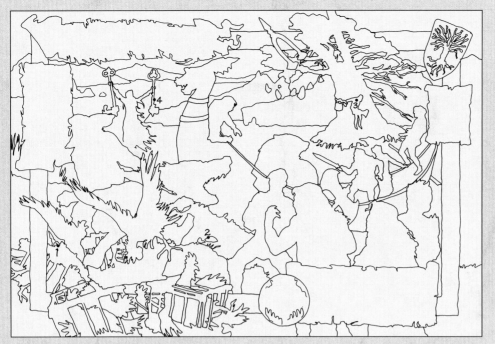

The Ferryman 18–19

Golden spur 1

Chalice 2

Missing knight: Sir Larbre 3

Correct key 4

Riddle answer:

Step 1. Take the wolf across to the island and row back.

Step 2. Take the hens across to the island and bring the wolf back.

Step 3. Leave the wolf on the mainland and take the bear across to the island.

Step 4. Take the wolf across to the island.

Dragon's Cave 20–21

Golden shoe 1

Chalice 2

Route to key tower 3

Missing knight: Sir Nocturne. Route to his tower 4

Key tower 5

Sir Nocturne's tower 6

Route out of cave 7

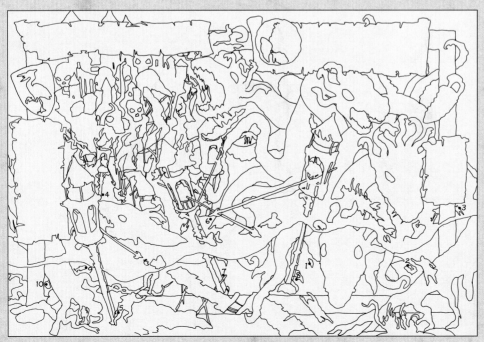

Monstrous Moat 22–23

Golden shoe 1

Chalice 2

Missing knight: Sir Heronbow 3

Levers 4 5 6 7 8

Glowing fish 9

Net 10

The Sorceress 24–25

Golden sword 1

Chalices 2 3 4
5 6 7 8 9 10

Sir Galahad's chalice 11

Correct shrine 12

The Round Table 26–27

Sir Lomvert 1
Chair C1

Sir Swinage 2
Chair C2

Sir Aquatane 3
Chair C3

Sir Gawain 4
Chair C4

Sir Tripont 5
Chair C5

Sir Larbre 6
Chair C6

Sir Nocturne 7
Chair C7

Sir Heronbow 8
Chair C8

Sir Galahad 9
Chair C9

Lady Lionheart 10
Chair C10

Hal Hirsuit 11
Chair C11

Guy Lowman 12
Chair C12

Beast in a circle
of light 13

Living beast 14

Woven symbol 15

Excalibur 16

Reader's chair 17

Did you also see these strange sights?

~ a lizard with six legs in Raven's Wood?

~ a man with a saucepan on his head at Swine Hill?

~ a monkey with wings on Fool's Lake?

~ a skull at the Demon's Bridge?

~ a ram's head in the Chapel of the Green Knight?

~ the ferryman's bad foot?

~ a lucky duck who escaped the cooking pot at the Round Table?

Thank you!